DATE DUE

MAR 1 8	FEB 2 1
APR 0 7	MAR 0 1
APR 1 5	SEP 2 7
MAY 1 6	MAR 1 4
NOV 1 8	
FEB 1 2	MAR 0 4
MAR 2 2	
APR 0 7	MAR 2 5
DEC 1 6	
FEB 0 2	OCT 3 0
FEB 1 6	JAN 0 4
APR 1 3	
NOV 0 7	MAR / 5
JAN 1 1	
FEB 0 3	

I WANT TO DO MAGIC
Simple Magic
Peter Eldin

Copper Beech Books
Brookfield, Connecticut

© Aladdin Books Ltd 2002
Produced by
Aladdin Books Ltd
28 Percy Street
London W1T 2BZ

ISBN 0–7613–2753–3

First published in the United States in 2002 by
Copper Beech Books,
an imprint of
The Millbrook Press
2 Old New Milford Road
Brookfield, Connecticut 06804

Designers:
Flick, Book Design & Graphics
Pete Bennett

Editor:
Leen De Ridder

Illustrators:
Catherine Ward, Peter Wilks—SGA
Tony Kenyon—BL Kearley

Printed in U.A.E.

Cataloging-in-Publication data is on file
at the Library of Congress

The author, Peter Eldin, is a professional magician.

Photo credits
Abbreviations: l-left, r-right, b-bottom, t-top, c-center, m-middle
All pictures supplied by Select Pictures except for:
15br, 27br—All Star Picture Library.
21b, 23br—Mary Evans Picture Library.

Contents

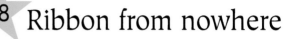

Introduction

Magic is the art of doing tricks that defy the laws of nature. Magic is a great hobby and will let you amaze and entertain your family and friends. All the tricks in *Simple Magic* use everyday materials, and are easy to learn. You don't need any special skills to be able to do them.

How to learn tricks

1. Read through the whole trick twice. It is alright if you do not understand everything at this stage.

2. Gather all the things you need.

3. Go through the trick again, doing the actions step by step.

4. If you are not comfortable with a particular action, see if you can adapt it to suit you better.

5. You can now start practicing the various movements, making sure that your hands are in the right place and that you can move smoothly from one step to another.

6. Once you have practiced the moves, you can start rehearsing the trick (performing it as if for a real audience).

7. When you are happy that you can perform the trick perfectly, try it out on your friends.

DID YOU KNOW...

... that in these circles you can find out lots of interesting facts about the props you use?

Top Tip

Watch out for this symbol to read some top tips! They will help you take a trick further or give you useful extra information.

Magicians and their magic
In boxes like this one, you will find information about famous magicians and their tricks.

IT'S **MAGIc**

HINTS

- Never repeat a trick in the same company. The first showing of a trick amazes the audience. Do it again and they will know what is coming. The element of surprise is gone and the trick will not be as enjoyable. Because the audience knows what is coming the second time around, it is also easier for them to figure out how the trick is done.

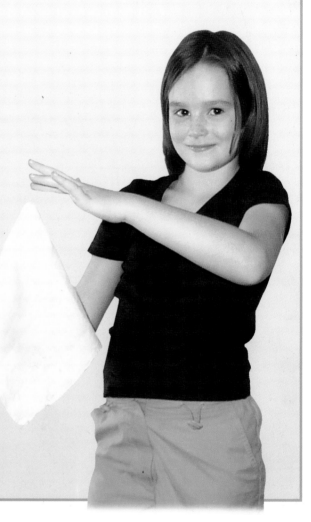

- Your success as a magician will depend a lot on the way you present a trick. Even the simplest trick can look fantastic if you perform it confidently and without hesitating. This may sound like a strange piece of advice, but your performance of magic will improve if you believe that what you are doing is really magic. Believe you are doing real magic and you will be!

- When people ask how your tricks are done, do not tell them. Although many people may ask, they will be disappointed when you let them know how simple some tricks really are. Keep the secrets secret!

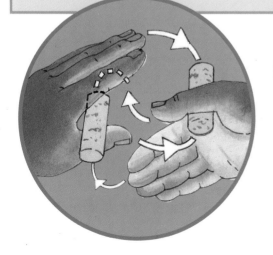

ⓘ These exclamation marks tell you what to watch out for in certain tricks or in the preparation for them. They may look like unimportant details when you first read them, but you may give away the trick if you ignore them.

Follow my eggsample

THE TRICK

Show your magic talents by balancing an ordinary egg on one end. When someone else tries to do it, they will always fail!

Preparation

> **You will need:**
> • an egg
> • some salt
> • a tablecloth

1 Before you begin, lay the tablecloth over the table.

2 Secretly put a small amount of salt in the palm of your left hand.

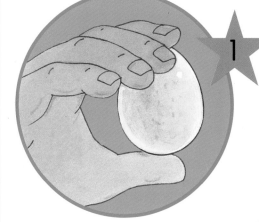

1 Show the egg to your audience. Hand it to someone to check that it is just an ordinary egg.

While the egg is being examined, secretly wet the tip of your right thumb with your tongue.

2

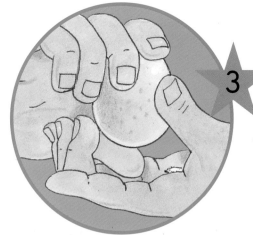

3 Take the egg back in your right hand and rub your wet thumb along its base.

The egg bag

Tricks with eggs have been around a long time. A Polish-born magician called Arnold de Biere (1876-1934) once had a famous trick called "the egg bag" in his shows. He used a small cloth bag which seemed to be empty, then amazed his audience by making several eggs appear and disappear from the bag.

IT'S **mAGIc**

4

Ask someone to check that there is nothing unusual about the tablecloth. As they do this, rest the egg on your left palm. This makes some of the salt stick to it.

Top Tip

To emphasize the fact that you are using just an ordinary egg for this trick, you could let someone in the audience pick any egg from a box of eggs. After you have finished the trick, you could even crack it in a bowl and show the audience the shell, egg white, and yolk. Nothing special about this egg!

Carefully balance the egg on the table. The salt helps keep the egg upright, but because there is so little of it, it cannot be seen.

5

Pick up the egg and hand it to someone else to try the trick, at the same time wiping the salt off the bottom. Try as they might, nobody will be able to balance the egg on its end!

6

7

Corkscrew

THE TRICK

Baffle your audience by making two corks pass through one another. This great penetration trick will astound everyone who sees it!

Preparation

You will need:
• 2 corks

There is no secret preparation needed for this trick; you just need to practice.

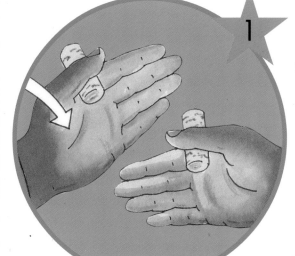

1 Put one cork in the thumb fold of the left hand and one in the thumb fold of the right hand.

2 Place your right thumb tip on the left cork at the end nearest the palm, with your right middle finger touching the other end of the same cork. Without letting go of the corks, turn your left finger in toward you. Now you can hold the right cork between your middle finger and thumb of your left hand, with the thumb nearest to your right palm.

DID YOU KNOW...

... that cork is made from the bark of the cork oak tree? The bark is stripped away every 8 to 10 years without damaging the tree.

3 Let the audience look at your hands for a second or two. The corks and hands will appear to be interlocked.

Now separate your hands with a slight twisting movement. Make sure this movement is quick and do it with a lot of confidence, so that your audience can't work out what happened. It will look as if the corks have passed through one another.

4

Top Tip

It is a good idea to practice in front of a mirror. That way, you can see what the audience will see, and you can check if your trick looks convincing. To pull off this trick successfully, you need to make sure that the hands and corks look interlocked. If you find it hard to place your fingers correctly, you can try and do the trick in reverse order first. Hold a cork between the thumb and middle finger of each hand, and put it into the thumb fold of the other hand. By working your way back from the end result to the beginning, you may find it easier to see how to hold your hands.

Move your hands apart, show the audience the two separate corks and take a bow!

5

Bend, bend, bend

THE TRICK

Your friends and family will love this clever trick. Bend a spoon and then make it straight again by using your fantastic magic powers.

Preparation

You will need:
• a spoon—make sure you can cover the handle with both hands.

No secret preparation needed.

Pick up the spoon in your left hand, holding it by its handle. Close your fingers around it.

Place the bowl of the spoon on the table. The bowl should be in front of your hand and the handle should be behind it.

Bring your right hand over to sit on the whole of your left hand. Secretly stick your left little finger under the handle near to the bowl.

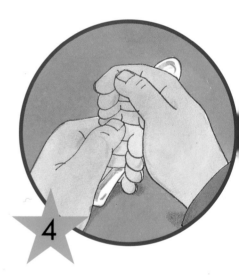

Pretend to be using some effort as you now move your hands forward to an upright position. Make sure the spoon does not move, with the handle staying hidden behind your hands.

Famous spoons
Probably the most famous person associated with spoon bending is the Israeli performer, Uri Geller (born 1946). He bends spoons and other objects using the power of his mind. He can even bend things in your living room while you watch him on TV!

IT'S mAGIc

Keep the spoon on the table and start moving your hands back and forth, as if you are bending the spoon more easily now. Because the handle is still hidden, everyone will think that the spoon is being bent.

5

Now bring your hands flat onto the table, over the spoon. Pretend to straighten the spoon.

6

Show the straight spoon to the audience. They will be amazed to see it completely unharmed!

7

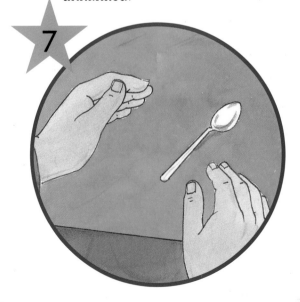

Top Tip

Once you can do this trick convincingly, try and do it again holding a small silver coin between your thumb and fingers (see below). Allow a small part of the coin to stick out when you pretend to bend the spoon, and it will look like the top of the spoon. You will need to practice holding the coin beforehand without showing it.

11

Vanishing spoon

THE TRICK

Pick up a spoon, bend it a bit, then make it disappear completely from your hands! This is a good trick to perform at a party or dinner table.

Preparation

You will need:
• a spoon; make sure you can hide it between your hands (see step 2).

No secret preparation needed, but you must be seated at a table for this trick.

Pick up the spoon with the tip of the handle between the first and second fingers of your right hand and the bowl between the first and second fingers of your left hand.

Say you are going to bend the spoon. Bring your hands together so the fingertips touch and the whole of the spoon is now hidden behind your hands.

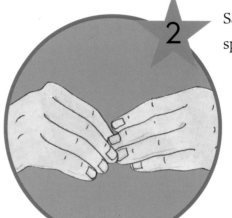

Hold the spoon about 6 inches (15 cm) above the table top and start moving your hands back and forth as if you are bending the spoon.

Top Tip

You can take this trick one stage further if you wish, provided that there is no carpet in the room you are in. As soon as the spoon has vanished (step 7), stop just for an instant and then loudly bang your hands down onto the table.

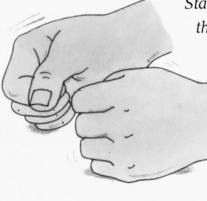

Stand up to do this and the spoon will fall from your lap and clatter onto the floor. Your audience will be amazed to see you have made the spoon pass right through the solid table.

4 Look at one of the spectators and say that the spoon is rather tough. At the same time, allow your hands to drop to the table.

You must now do two things at once. Raise your hands, keeping them together. At the same time, secretly drop the spoon from your fingers onto your lap. You have now ditched the spoon.

5

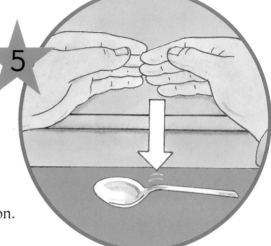

Make sure your legs are closed so the spoon doesn't fall onto the ground.

6 Move your hands sharply as though breaking the spoon in two. You must act as though you are still holding the spoon.

Open your hands to look at the break and act really surprised that the spoon has vanished!

7

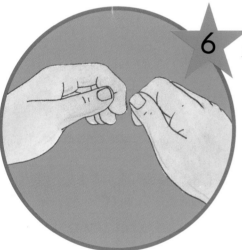

Practice standing up at the right moment. The spoon should clatter to the floor right after you bang your hands on the table.

Changing color

THE TRICK

Amaze your audience by making a red magic wand change to black.

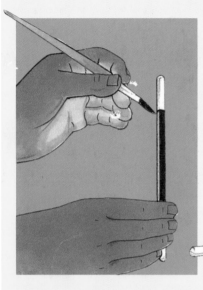

2 Cut the red colored paper to the same length as the black part of your magic wand.

Preparation

You will need:
- red colored paper
- a wooden dowel, about 8 inches long
- glue
- black paint
- white paint
- a newspaper

1 First, paint a dowel black with white ends, as shown in the picture. This will be your traditional black magic wand.

3 Roll the paper around the wand and glue it to make a paper tube. It is a good idea to make several of these tubes at the same time if you plan to do this trick a lot.

Hold up the wand with the paper tube covering the black part so it looks like a red wand.

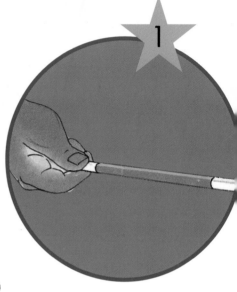

Wrap the wand in the newspaper, leaving the white ends poking out. If you like, you can say some magic words or wave your wand for extra effect.

Hold the wand tight and pull it out of the newspaper. The paper tube stays hidden inside the newspaper, and it looks as if the wand has changed color.

3

4

Casually wad up the newspaper and drop it on the table or floor as you take a bow.

A change of course

A young man who wanted to become a ventriloquist went into a magic shop to buy a ventriloquist's dummy. As a result of that visit, he became interested in magic, studied hard, and is now the most famous magician in the world —David Copperfield (born 1956) (below). From walking through the Great Wall of China to making the Statue of Liberty vanish, no illusion seems impossible for him!

Chameleon thimble

THE TRICK

Wave a handkerchief over a thimble on your fingertip and make it magically change color!

Preparation

You will need:
- a thimble
- a second thimble, larger and different in color
- a handkerchief

Before you start, put the small thimble inside the large one.

Hold up the large thimble on your finger. The audience must not know about the hidden thimble.

1

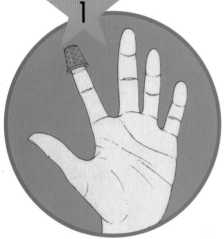

Drape the handkerchief over the thimble.

2

Now lift the handkerchief, lifting off the large thimble at the same time.

3

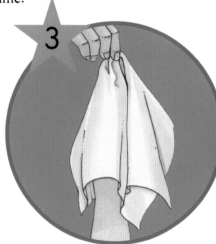

Let everyone see that the thimble on your finger has changed color. Keep the large thimble hidden in the handkerchief.

4

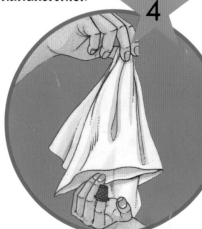

Utter nonsense

Magicians used to use special magic words to make their tricks seem more mysterious. At the start of each trick, one magician in the 1700s used to say, "Hocus pocus, tontus, talontus, vade celeriter iubeo." It may have sounded impressive to the audience, but it was actually complete and utter nonsense!

IT'S **mAGIc**

Magnetic dice

THE TRICK

This is a fun trick where you can use your amazing magic powers to magnetize dice so that they stick together.

Preparation

You will need:
• 2 small dice

This trick works best with small dice, so make sure the ones you use are not too heavy.

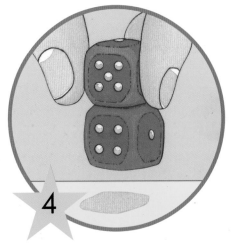

4

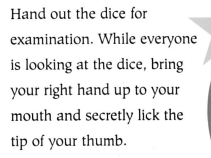

1

Hand out the dice for examination. While everyone is looking at the dice, bring your right hand up to your mouth and secretly lick the tip of your thumb.

To everyone's amazement, you now hold only the top die and the bottom one stays stuck to it.

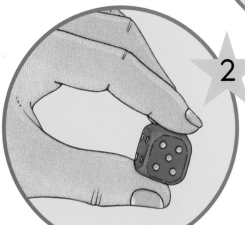

2

Take the dice back and rub your wet thumb over the bottom face of one of them.

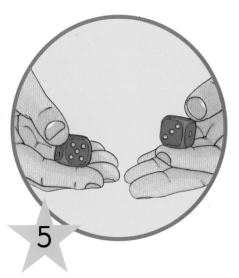

5

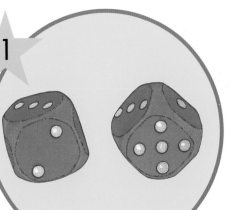

3

Place this die on top of the other one, saying that you are going to magnetize them.

Pull the dice apart and hand them out for examination. As you do this, secretly wipe your thumb over the top of the lower die and the bottom of the upper die to dry off any moisture still remaining.

Ribbon from nowhere

THE TRICK

Baffle your audience by putting your empty hands together and then producing a long ribbon... from nowhere!

Preparation

You will need:
- a long ribbon
- a magic wand

1 Before you begin, roll the ribbon around one end of the wand.

2 Place the wand behind something on your table.

Show your empty hands to the audience.

1

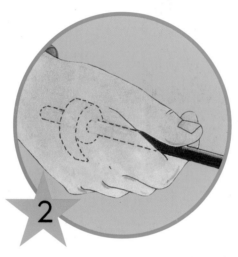

2

Pick up the magic wand with your right hand. As you do so, place your hand over the ribbon, hiding it from view.

Tap the end of the wand against the palm of your left hand.

3

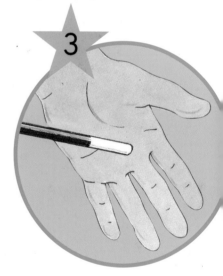

DID YOU KNOW...

... that magic wands always used to be black and white? Now, many magicians use a colored one, or even a pencil or chopsticks!

Close your hand and tap the wand against it again.

4

18

5 Open your left hand to show that it is empty.

6 Now use your left hand to pull the wand from the right fist, leaving the ribbon hidden in your right hand.

7 Tap your right hand with the wand and put the wand back on your table.

8 Bring both hands together, pause for a second, then dramatically pull the ribbon out between your hands!

Top Tip

This trick will also look very impressive if you use a handkerchief instead of a ribbon. Fold the handkerchief over and over to form a flat strip (see below), then wind it around the end of the wand. Follow the steps described above, and pull it out with a flourish. You can use anything for this trick that can be made small enough to fit in your hand, and that looks impressive when you pull it out.

Chewing gum fun

THE TRICK

In this fun trick, a spectator tries to guess which of your closed hands holds a stick of chewing gum, but is proved wrong every time. On the last guess the gum vanishes completely!

Preparation

> **You will need:**
> • a pack of chewing gum sticks

Take the pack of gum from your side pocket or wallet and ask a spectator to pull out a stick.

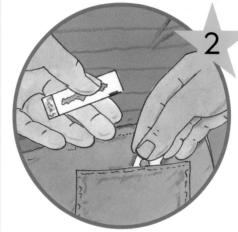

Hold the stick behind your back and tell the spectator that she can have it if she can guess which hand it is in. As you are saying this, secretly pull the other stick of gum from its hiding place.

Bring your hands to the front, closed, with a stick of gum in each hand. Ask the spectator to guess which hand holds the gum.

1 Before you do this trick, you need to slide a stick of gum under the back of your belt or put it in a back pocket.

2 Put the rest of the pack in a side pocket or a wallet.

IT'S **mAGIc**

Devised in a dream
One of the most spectacular illusions invented by the great British magician David Devant (1868-1941) was called "the mascot moth." An assistant was dressed to look like a moth.

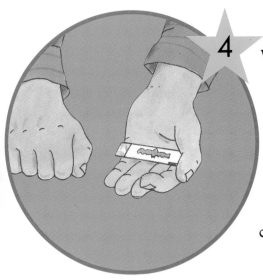

4 Whichever hand she picks, you say, "No, you are wrong. The gum is here!" And you open the other hand to show the gum. Put your hands behind your back once again and give the spectator another chance. Do exactly the same as before—have a stick of gum in each hand, but open the hand not chosen to show the gum.

Offer to give the spectator one more chance. Put your hands behind your back and this time secretly put both sticks of gum under your belt or in a back pocket. **5**

6 Bring your closed hands to the front and ask which hand holds the gum. This time, open the hand that is chosen, but show that it is empty.

Then open the other hand as well. It is also empty—the gum has vanished! **7**

She suddenly vanished when the magician approached with a candle. The inspiration for this trick came to Devant in a dream. In this photo, David Devant is shown with his sister, doing a trick where he makes her float in the air. This is called levitation.

Impossible escape

THE TRICK

You and your assistant are tied together at the wrists. Escape seems impossible without untying the ribbons, but within seconds you are separated and neither of the ribbons has been untied.

Preparation

You will need:
• 2 ribbons or soft ropes, each about 4 feet long.

There is no preparation needed.

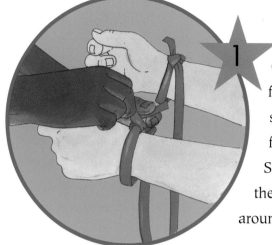

1 Call your assistant forward or ask for someone to come up from the audience. Show the ribbons and tie the two ends of one of them around the assistant's wrists.

If you take someone from the audience, be aware that she will know how the trick is done afterward.

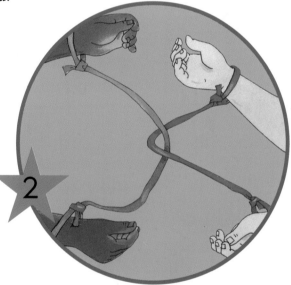

2

Ask your assistant to tie the other ribbon around your wrists in the same way, but to link the center of the two rings before doing so. The two of you now seem inseparable. Ask the audience if anyone wants to try separating you without untying any knots. Nobody will be able to!

Top Tip

With practice, you will be able to do these movements very quickly. The quicker you can do them, the more impossible the escape will seem, and the more impressed your audience will be! If you want to practice the moves without having to tie up a friend every time, you can tie yourself to a chair and master the moves like that.

Take the center of your ribbon and push it under the ribbon around your assistant's right wrist. The direction in which you do this is important—you must push it through from the assistant's arm and toward the wrist.

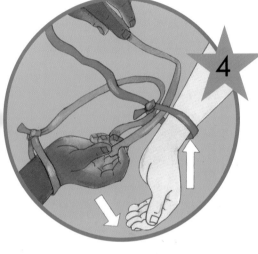

Pass the loop over your assistant's hand and then back through the wrist loop, this time going from the finger side toward the arm.

To your audience's amazement, the two loops will now be free of one another.

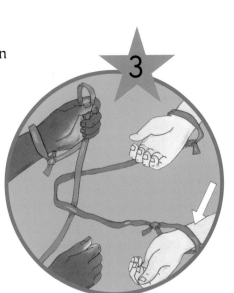

Rope of mystery

Possibly the most famous trick in the history of magic is a suspension trick called the Indian rope trick. In one version of this, a rope is thrown in the air, where it remains suspended. A small boy then climbs up the rope. When he reaches the top, he vanishes and the rope falls to the ground. It certainly is a remarkable trick. And the most remarkable thing about it is that it never existed! It is merely a travelers' tale. So this photo—like all magic— is make believe.

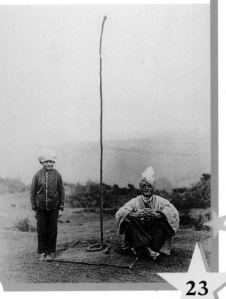

The ghost

Reach into your pocket and take out the handkerchief. Pull out the tape measure at the same time. Palm the tape measure—make sure you keep it hidden in your hand.

Hold the handkerchief at the top corners by the first finger and thumb of each hand.

2

3

Cross your hands over to show the other side of the handkerchief. Remember to keep the tape measure hidden.

Drape the handkerchief over your right hand and immediately pull up the center into a peak.

4

1

5

Keep pulling the center of the handkerchief up. You should be able to get it standing quite high before it drops down again. Now do the same again, but this time get hold of the end of the tape through the material. Lift the center of the handkerchief and the hidden tape as high as it will go without it showing from under the handkerchief.

24

6 Let go with your left hand and the handkerchief remains upright as if supported by a ghost.

7 Bring your left hand to the top of the handkerchief and push it down, pushing the tape measure down at the same time.

8 Once again, open up the handkerchief and show it on both sides as you did before, keeping the tape measure hidden in your right hand. Fold the handkerchief and put it back into your pocket, putting the secret tape measure away in the pocket at the same time.

! **Make sure your tape measure doesn't "talk" when you do this trick. If it makes a noise, your audience will become suspicious.**

IT'S **mAGIc**

Splendid silks

Many famous—and not-so-famous—magicians perform tricks with silks in their shows. In one very popular trick, two handkerchiefs are tied together. A third handkerchief, usually of a contrasting color to the others, is first vanished by the magician and then it reappears tied between the knotted handkerchiefs.

Orders, please!

THE TRICK

In this amazing trick, you pour some water into a pitcher. When you pour it out again, it will have magically changed into real milk!

1 First put the plastic cup into the pitcher. Pack the sponge against the cup to hold it in place. You may need to add some more sponge, foam, or even scrunched-up paper to keep everything firmly in place.

Preparation

You will need:
- a glass
- a plastic cup
- a sponge
- water and milk
- a pitcher

2 Pour the milk into the plastic cup.

3 Now, pour some water into the glass. Put all your props on a table.

Show the glass of water to the audience, then pour it into the pitcher. You actually pour it onto the sponge, which will absorb it. Be careful not to pour any of the water into the cup of milk.

Now tip the pitcher and pour the milk out into the glass. It looks as if you have made the water turn into milk!

Make sure nobody in the audience can see what is hidden in the pitcher!

Hand the glass to someone in the audience so that they can taste it to make sure that it is real milk.

3

Liquid magic
Tricks with liquids are very popular with magicians. David Devant had a magic kettle that poured any drink called for. Magician Milton Woodward had a whole act called Wonder Bar, in which he produced numerous drinks. British magician Paul Daniels (born 1938) (below) now owns David Devant's original magic kettle and also performs tricks with liquids in his shows.

Top Tip

To make this trick even more spectacular, you can prepare several pitchers with different liquids. In this way, you can turn water into milk into orange juice, for example. You could also make a drink list, with the different drinks you have in the prepared pitchers. You can then change water into whatever drink your audience picks—as long as it is on the list, of course!

27

Chain of clips

THE TRICK

In this stunning trick, show five ordinary paper clips to the audience, then tip them into an empty bowl. When you take them out, your audience will be amazed to see that the clips have linked themselves together by magic!

Preparation

You will need:
- 10 paper clips
- a book (hardcover)
- a small bowl

1 Link five clips together and push them into the spine of the book. If you use colored paper clips, make sure that the ones in the chain are the same color as the single ones.

2 Put the book on your table, open at the middle pages.

3 Put the five loose clips into the bowl.

Tip the loose clips from the bowl into your hand. (This proves that the bowl is otherwise empty without you having to draw any special attention to the fact).

Count the clips one at a time onto the book to show that they are all separate.

Pick up the book and, keeping it low down, tip the clips back into the bowl. The linked clips will also fall into the bowl from their secret hiding place in the book spine.

Wave your hands over the bowl in a mysterious manner and then pick up the first clip in the chain.

4

Pull out the chain of clips, leaving the loose clips hidden in the bowl, as your audience applauds.

5

Top Tip

You can use the same idea to make money multiply. Secretly hide two coins in the book spine. Borrow two coins from people in the audience, put them on the book, and tip them into the bowl. At the same time, the coins you put in the spine of the book will fall out. Take out the four coins, and return the borrowed coins to their owners. Put the two extra ones into your pocket and say that this is the way magicians make money!

Bag of mystery

THE TRICK

A ribbon is cut into pieces and dropped into a bag. When you use your magic powers and remove it from the bag, it is in one piece again.

1 Place the three pieces of material one on top of another and sew them together on three sides. You now have a bag with two pockets in it.

Preparation

> You will need:
> • three matching pieces of material, measuring 7 by 8 inches
> • a needle and thread
> • 2 identical ribbons
> • scissors

2 Put one of the ribbons in the back pocket of the bag. This is called a load.

Give a pair of scissors and the ribbon to someone in the audience, and tell him to cut it into as many pieces as he likes.

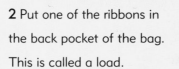

Put the pieces of ribbon into the bag, making sure they go into the front pocket of the bag.

Torn and restored newspaper
There are many different kinds of trick where something is torn or broken, and then restored. One of the most famous tricks using this idea is the one where a newspaper is torn to pieces. The magician then joins the pieces back together to form a complete newspaper.

IT'S **MAGIC**

Wave your hands over the bag and then reach into the back pocket.

3

Pull out the complete ribbon and it looks as if you have restored it to one piece by magic!

4

Top Tip

The magic bag can be used for lots of different tricks. Here are some you could try. In all of these tricks, whatever is put into the bag goes in the front compartment, and whatever is taken out has been placed secretly in the rear compartment before the show.

• A ribbon is dropped into the bag. When you take it out, there are several knots in it.

• A picture of a girl in a dirty dress is put into the bag. When she comes out, she is beautifully dressed.

• A ribbon and some buttons are put into the bag. When you pull out the ribbon, the buttons have been sewn onto it.

• Several rings are put into the bag. They link themselves together in the bag into a long chain.

• Several cards bearing letters of the alphabet are dropped into the bag. They come out linked together to spell a message like THE END, or the name of someone in the audience. Make sure you know someone's name beforehand.

MICHAEL

31

Index

Glossary of magic words

Ditch:
When you secretly get rid of something without the audience being aware of it.

Levitation:
When something or someone seems to float in the air.

Load:
When you hide an item beforehand and produce it later.

Palm:
When you secretly hold something in your hand.

Penetration:
When one solid thing seems to pass through another.

Suspension:
When something or someone hangs in the air looking as if it is attached to nothing.

Talk:
An accidental noise made by a hidden object which gives away its presence.

Web sites and clubs

Have you caught the magic bug and want to know more?

Here are some magic Web sites you could visit:
Magic tricks can be bought from:
•www.merlinswakefield.co.uk
•www.internationalmagic.com
•www.magictricks.com

• www.magicsam.com
Site of the Society of American Magicians. At age 100 this is the oldest magical society in the world.
• www.magicsym.org
Site of The Society of Young Magicians.
•www.magicyouth.com
Site of the youth program of the International Brotherhood of Magicians.